Valentines

ST. VALENTINE'S DAY.

Valentines

A Loving Remembrance

Jean P. Favalora
Lark Books

To my husband Frank, a heartfelt thank you for your support, encouragement, love, and interest.

ⓒ⊃

Published in 1995 by Lark Books
50 College Street
Asheville, North Carolina, U.S.A. 28801

© 1995 by Jean P. Favalora

Editor: Bobbe Needham
Design and production: Alex Alford
Photography: Len Wickens and Paul Smith

ISBN 0-937274-92-5

Library of Congress Cataloging-in-Publication Data
Favalora, Jean P.
    Valentines : a loving remembrance / by Jean P. Favalora
        p.   cm.
    Includes bibliographical references.
    ISBN 0-937274-92-5
    1. Valentines. 2. Greeting cards—United States. I. Title.
NC1866.V3F38   1995
741.6'84—dc20   95-30158
                           CIP

Contents

Preface

References

Preface

❧

I thank everyone who has encouraged me by their interest in my valentine collection, and I especially thank Kim Rich of Hallmark Cards, Kansas City, Missouri, and Denise Becker of Gibson Greetings, Inc., Cincinnati, Ohio, for answering my questions. A special thanks also to David Cox of Gloucester, Massachusetts, for his interest through the years and for information that led me to some fine valentines. Finally, I thank individuals who have allowed me to include their cards and those who have given me valentines for the collection: Ruth Anderson, Joseph Cody, David Cox, Norman Cox, Amy Favalora, Nona Favazza, Winnie and Dick Figurido, Ella Grant, Faye MacDonald, Elsie Marks, Anthony Pratt, Julia Rose, Clara Sears, and Katherine Souza. I thank my editor, Bobbe Needham, for her help and for recognizing the timeless appeal of valentines.

❧

I have identified the valentines by decade and maker wherever possible, although often even this must be an educated guess or rough estimate because popular designs were widely copied. Unless noted otherwise in a credit line, all the valentines and other items pictured are part of my own collection.

I am grateful to the following for their kind permission to include photographs of valentines from their collections; sources are indicated with each photo: the Cape Ann Historical Association, Gloucester, Massachusetts; the Manchester Historical Society, Manchester-by-the-Sea, Massachusetts; the Mount Holyoke College Library/Archives, South Hadley, Massachusetts; and the Society for the Preservation of New England Antiquities, Boston.

I wrote this book to share with you my collection of valentines, which has brought me great joy, and to remind us all of less complicated, more innocent times.

Of Saints and Lovers

1880s illustration of Valentinus

George C. Whitney Co. 1880 valentine's verse reads: "Virtue lives forever / In the mind, / In her alone true / Happiness we find."

As anyone whose heart has leapt or languished on February 14 might suspect, many legends surround those declarations of love we call valentines. One of them tells us that in Rome, on that date in about the year A.D. 269, Valentinus, a Christian priest, was martyred for love—though not exactly his own. The emperor, Claudius II, had decreed that Roman soldiers should not marry; a home and family would only distract them from their duty. When Valentinus continued to officiate at marriages of young Romans, Claudius had him thrown into prison. A year later, when the imprisoned Valentinus still refused to agree to obey the law, Claudius ordered him clubbed, stoned, and beheaded. During his confinement, the legend goes, Valentinus restored the sight of his jailer's blind daughter and on the eve of his execution wrote her a farewell note.

He signed it, "Your Valentine." Several centuries later, Pope Gelasius proclaimed February 14 St. Valentine's Day.

It took the English and a Frenchman to make St. Valentine's Day a celebration of love and lovers. Early English poets marked February 14 as the day that birds chose their mates (before the calendar was changed in 1582, that date fell later in the spring). Geoffrey Chaucer wrote in the 1300s:

> *For this was on*
> *St. Valentine's Day,*
> *When every fowl cometh*
> *there to choose his mate.*

And Shakespeare has a character in *A Midsummer Night's Dream* comment about two human lovers in the woods:

> *St. Valentine is past;*
> *Begin these woodbirds*
> *but to couple now?*

The Frenchman was Charles, Duke of Orleans, who gets the credit from historians for starting the valentine tradition we know. Captured by the English during the Battle of Agincourt in 1415, Charles sent his wife a love note from his prison room in the Tower of London on February 14. One of his verses expresses sentiments not too different from those in some of today's valentines:

> *Wilt thou be mine?*
> *dear love, reply,*
>
> *Sweet consent,*
> *or else deny:*
>
> *Whisper softly,*
> *none shall know,*
>
> *Wilt thou be mine, love?*
> *ay or no?*

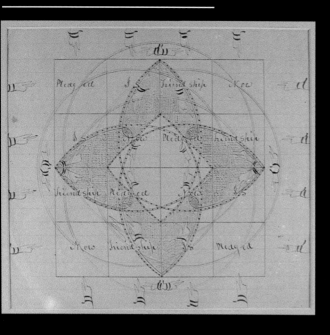

A hand-drawn friendship pledge that doubled as a game, early 1800s

Hand-written and passionate, c. 1845

Love for Sale

By the early 1700s, tongue-tied friends or lovers could turn to valentine writers' booklets like the Ladies' and Gentlemen's New and Original Valentine Writer by J. M. Fletcher of Nashua, New Hampshire. Often sold for a penny each, the guides offered a lyrical sampling of verses and poems for all of love's seasons. The writer of the lace valentine here chose a popular verse:

> Sweet is the dream divinely sweet
> When absent souls in fancy meet,
> At midnight love I'll think of Thee!
> At midnight love oh! think of me.

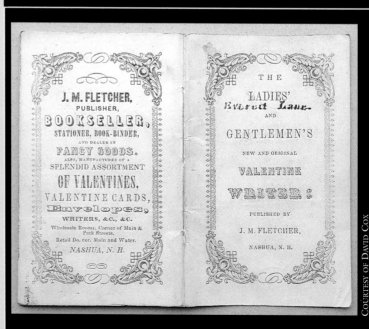

Most early American valentines combined imagination with love and friendship in the form of handmade acrostics, rebuses, puzzle purses, cutouts, and pin-prick designs. Puzzle purses were made from a sheet of paper cleverly folded to produce a square flat envelope in the center, which often carried a ring or gift. On the purse Elisha Shear gave Eunice Haskins of Shutesbury, Massachusetts, on March 28, 1811, he wrote a love poem around the square:

My Dear these Lines
to you I Rite
to send to you my harts Delight
and When these lines come
Whare you dwell
I hope that thay
may find you Well...
If you Will With me
join hand and hand
and [rescue?] me from
love['s] cruel bands

ile come and Take you
in my arms
and all Ways
Will adore your charms.
My love this is true
Nothing but death
shall part me from you.

Elisha Shear's puzzle purse

Wearing Your Heart
on Your Sleeve

In eighteenth-century England, and so perhaps in America, the mystery of who their future husbands would be seemed to preoccupy many single women on Valentine's Day. One custom was to write men's names on pieces of paper, roll these in clay, and drop them all like beads into water. The true sweetheart's name would rise to the surface first. In another custom of the time, men drew women's names from a jar to choose their valentines, to whom they then owed special favors and gifts ranging from a pair of gloves to an elaborate ball. Among one group of friends, the men wore their valentine's name on their sleeve, perhaps the origin of a phrase we still use.

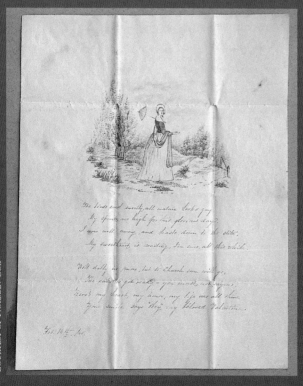

Hand-drawn cards, mid-1800s

Men of the time sometimes proposed marriage by sending woven valentines whose elaborate designs were probably of Pennsylvania German origin. These often showed interlocking hearts and hands or endlessly looping spirals of lines and words in which the last phrase led back to the first—a real lovers' knot.

A proposal? Scissor-cut card with interlocking hearts, 1830s-1840s

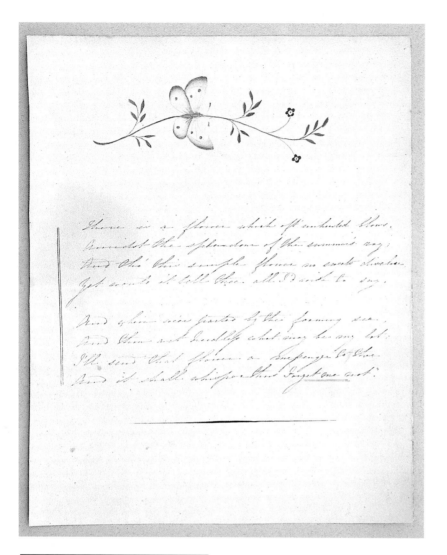

Whispering "Forget me not," c. 1845

Valentine artists have loved butterflies and forget-me-nots for at least 150 years, almost as much as they love flowery sentiments, like these passionate verses from 1845:

> *There is a flower*
> *which oft' unheeded blows*
> *Amidst the splendour*
> *of the summer's ray*
> *And though this simple flower*
> *no sweets disclose*
> *Yet wants it tell thee*
> *all I'd wish to say.*
>
> *And when we're parted*
> *by the foaming sea,*
> *And thou art heedless*
> *that may be my lot,*
> *I'll send that flower*
> *a messenger to thee*
> *And it shall whisper this*
> *"Forget me not."*

Of Queens and Cupids

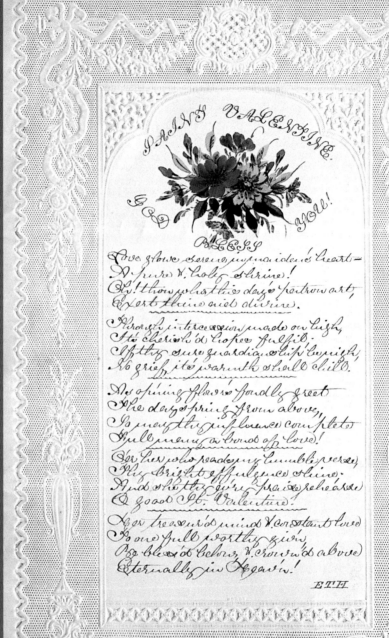

Lacy creation by Joseph Mansell, 1850s

The young Queen Victoria, who ascended the British throne in 1837, believed in making occasions of anniversaries, weddings, children's birthdays, and holidays in general. Perhaps her point of view set the royal seal of approval on the sending of valentines—some of the first commercial valentines came from England, from the workshops of Joseph Addenbrooke and H. Dobbs, paper manufacturers and embossers, and a little later, from Joseph Mansell, an engraver and maker of fancy stationery.

As embossed papers and paper lace became popular in the 1830s and 1840s, hand-drawn and hand-colored art and a handwritten message combined with the raised ornamentation of embossing to produce even more elegant and charming cards. Acrostic valentines that spelled out the beloved's name continued to be personal and unique gifts.

An early embossed lace valentine by Dobbs, 1840-45

"Flowers of affection" by Mansell, c. 1845

Mansell's "Affection's Offering," 1850s

Paper Lace

❧

Like many discoveries, the creation of paper lace happened by mistake. Joseph Addenbrooke, an Englishman, noticed on a bit of embossed paper left on a die press that some of the "bosses," or raised tips of paper, were missing. Filing off more of the bosses created a lacy effect … paper lace.

Typical paper lace, 1850s

An acrostic on embossed paper by Dobbs,
in French, c. 1832

In childhood when our hearts were young,
A tender feeling 'tween us sprung,
Which makes me send these lines to you
To tell you I continue true.

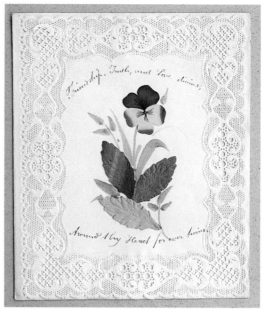

Mid 1800s miniature treasures, about 3 x 4-1/2"

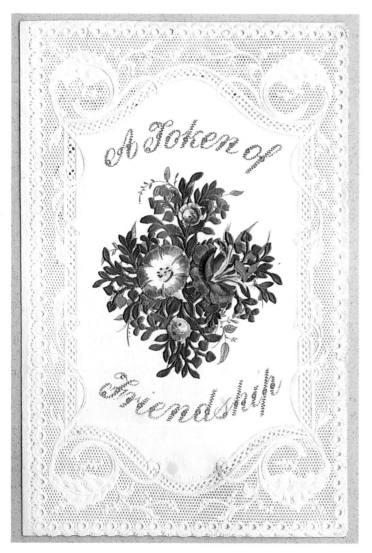

Typical 1850s elegance

Embossed lace envelope by Mansell, c. 1850

Early homemade envelope from trifolded sheet of paper, sealed with a dab of red wax, shows early hand canceling, February 14, 1846

In the years before 1845 and the first postal deliveries, every valentine in the United States was delivered by hand, usually folded and sealed with a dab of red wax. Tiny paper wafers also sealed the earliest envelopes, called "paper pockets," which didn't come into common use until almost the middle of the century.

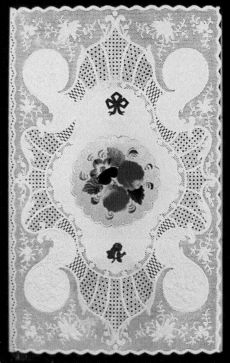

Mansell's best-known design, 1850s

FAREWELL

Farewell, farewell, although it break
My heart the cruel word to speak;
Yet well I know that you must go,
You, whom I have loved so.
My eyes are dim with bitter tears;
My heart is weak
with wasting fears;
My lips scarce speak
the bitter word,
The harshest sound
mine ears have heard.
Yet, it must be,
these sufferings tell,
That you must go;
farewell! farewell!

Mansell valentine, 1850s, carried a tragic sentiment.

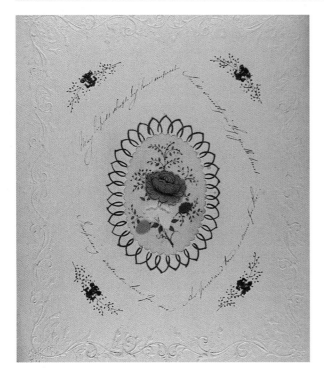

Flower center covered hidden message, c.1840

Acrostic lithograph, c. 1835

Elegant gold-finished envelope, hand-delivered February 14, 1852, in Allentown, Pennsylvania.

Fetching watercolor center adorns embossed mid-1800s card

y the 1840s, commercial woodcuts and lithographs had combined with lace-edged and embossed designs to usher in the golden era of valentines. Many people continued to draw and paint their own cards and handwrite poems in neat, curlicued letters. They often embellished bought cards with pasted arrangements of colorful flowers and leaves or with tiny manufactured gilt or aluminum stickers—musical notes, rings, and medallions.

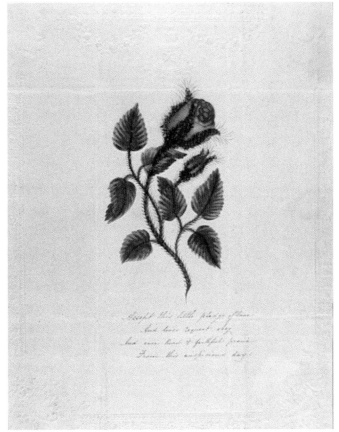

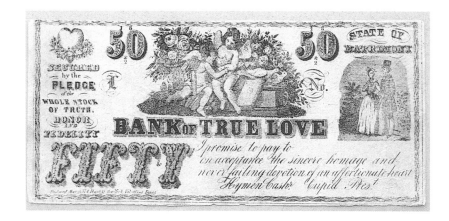

Novelty lithograph printed on bill-sized paper, 1852

Printed from flat, inked surfaces onto paper, early lithographs often showed finely drawn romantic scenes or figures. The busiest of the New York valentine publishers, lithographer T. W. Strong, also distributed comic valentines and valentine writers' booklets, beginning in 1842.

T. W. Strong lithograph, 4 x 7", 1850s

Sweet are the balmy drops that steal
When dusky eve her shades reveal,
But not more sweet—my hopes betide—
Than when—thou'rt seated by my side

I envy not—the princely grot,
'Tis cheerless all—where thou art not—
Oh! as my soul prays fervently
So may thy fond heart beat for me.

Hand-colored lithograph, c. 1845

Ah! to my bosom thou art dear,
    More dear than words can tell,
And if a fault is cherish'd there,
    'Tis loving thee too well.—

31

Penny Dreadfuls

The comic valentines of the mid-1800s to the early 1900s were more aptly known as "vinegar valentines" for their often stinging, frequently cruel messages. Those printed on cheap paper and sold for a penny were also called "penny dreadfuls." Their grotesque drawings caricatured common stereotypes: the fat and the skinny, the town drunkard, the inept seamstress, the crooked politician, the spinster schoolmarm.

This card, which lampoons overdressed women, manages to offend—at least—most women and older women in particular, all feminists, and housewives. The front of the card shows the woman dressed in satin, then opens to reveal her in kitchen clothes, mending a stocking.

I will not quarrel with thy dress so fine;
I'm only happy that you are not mine;
Although it grieves me very much to see
You dress'd in so much useless finery.
Sure, 't were better suited to your age
In some domestic duties to engage;
To stay at home and mend some holey stocking.
And not with flippancy the world be shocking
Forgetting on thy brow how old Time is knocking.

Flower-cage valentine by George Kershaw, an embosser and lace-paper maker, 1845-50

P opular during the same era were flower-cage valentines; pulling an invisible thread lifted a spiral-cut design to reveal the caged message hidden beneath.

Flower-cage valentine, c. 1845, whose hidden message reads "My heart I send to thee"

*Elaborate embossed
envelopes popular in
the 1860s*

TO MY SWEET
LOVE
All joy and bliss
Be ever thine
My idol love
My Valentine

My love
will never
Change

Embossed paper made love even sweeter, c.1855

Howland card, 2 x 3",
1850s or 1860s

Esther Howland, designed first U.S. valentines

Fifteen years before the U.S. Civil War, the woman who has been called the Daughter of the American Valentine began producing the layered, hand-cut, lacy cards that would eventually make her New England Valentine Company a booming assembly-line business. Esther Howland created her first valentines with fancy papers ordered from England by her father, a "fancy stationer" and bookseller in Worcester, Massachusetts. With no real expectations, she gave samples to her brother to take along with his regular load of books on his horse-and-buggy sales trip around the nearby states. When he arrived home with several thousand dollars' worth of orders, she immediately set up shop in an upstairs room of her father's home.

Howland card, showing red wafer behind church cut-out, 1870s

Howland card, book and figure glued on, 1865-75

Esther Howland turned the standard flat English lace valentine into a confection of layered lace, pictures, and hand-cut birds, leaves, and flowers. She designed accordion-pleated paper tabs to create three-dimensional designs, and she slipped brightly colored wafers behind paper lace to set off the delicate patterns. She was also the first to place verses on paper slips attached to the back page of a folded valentine. The verse inside her 1870s card shown here, which on the front promises "My sincere love to you," reads:

To thee, my love,
I give my heart,
I give me love to thee,
Cupid shall ne'er from us depart,
Though thou art far from me.

Howland graduated from Mount Holyoke Female Seminary, now Mount Holyoke College, whose library houses this "beehive" valentine.

In the early years of the business, friends and family members could be found in the Howland attic working late into the summer evenings, and in winter by gaslight, scissors clicking over Esther's designs. Slivers and coils of paper drifted around their feet like snow, in a landscape of paste pots, brushes, and jars of paint and boxes overflowing with paper scraps and pictures.

Single sheet, British factory-made card, c. 1850

Esther Howland's inspired creations grew more popular as the century matured. Valentines celebrated romance in America and England by becoming even more ornate and colorful, with more lace, more elaborate borders, more embossing, more bright inserts and stick-on decorations. Sometimes senders of valentines enclosed daguerreotypes or, later, tintypes of themselves — photographs on metal.

My peace with wild emotion's torn,
From morn to eve, from eve till morn.
And would you, fair one, care to know
The reason why I languish?
Tis you who've cost me all this woe,
This heart-ache and this anguish.
For dear, I love you deep and true,
And ne'er shall cease to think of you.

Daguerreotypes and tintypes like these often accompanied nineteenth-century valentines.

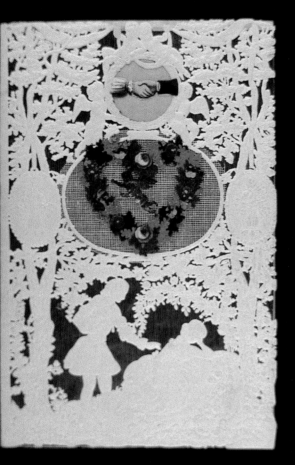

*Elaborate embossed cameo by
Kershaw & Son, c. 1860*

*Urn base is embossed with Joseph Mansell's name,
1860s. The verse inside reads: "If this accepted be by
you / Then ever be sincere and true / But if this
motto you decline / Then I am not your Valentine.*

Delicate lace of Mansell valentines repeated on lacy envelope, c. 1850

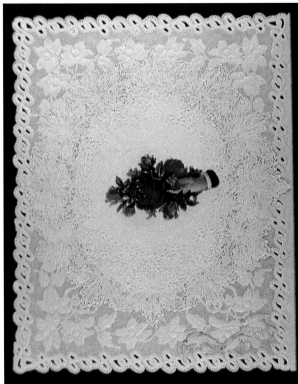

Cupid

❧

The chubby winged cherub with the bow and arrows who appears on many valentines started life as a handsome, athletic Roman god, the son of Mercury and Venus. (In Greece he was Eros.) In myths his dual nature combines cruelty and happiness—like love, he brings both pain and joy. According to legend, he sharpened his arrows on a grind-stone wetted with blood, and the romantics among us still say that someone in love has been wounded by one of Cupid's darts.

Leap Year Proposal.

I give you fair warning, that when next we meet,
Be it inside the house or out on the street.
I'm going to propose to you right on the spot,
And if you accept me oh, happy your lot.

Copyright, F. J. Bilek, Chicago, 1908.

LOVE'S TELEGRAM

Love's Telegram

HANDED IN AT _P.A.M._ RECEIVED AT _P.M._

To my
Sweetheart

Cupid's arrow's sorely smart,
Take them quick out of my heart,
Bring a potion of love's wine
To your own true Valentine

CUPID'S CABLE

DIVINITY AVENUE
FEB 14

THESE OFFICES ARE OPEN ON THE 14th OF FEB. FOR THE RECEIPT
AND DESPATCH OF MESSAGES OF LOVE ONLY.

THE CABLES ARE EVERYWHERE AND CONNECT LOVING HEARTS
ALL OVER THE WORLD.

HANDED IN AT CUPID CABLE STATION   9. A.M.

I'm all on thorns to know my fate so cabled
as I couldn't wait   now what I want
may be you'll guess   it's only this a little
                                                    yes

CUPID'S CABLE

Miss Maxim F. Wilcox
Brattleboro
7 Chapin St.   Vermont

Personalized Rock & Co.
valentine includes
monogram, 1860s

Of Seashells and Sachets

Civil War tent valentine, known as "Soldier Dreams of Home," 1860s;
envelope (sold separately) commemorates the heroes of two wars, "Officer
Warren, the first officer killed in the Revolution" and "Officer Ellsworth,
the first officer killed in the present Rebellion," 1861

The Weekly Novelette.

VOLUME X.—NUMBER 24.   BOSTON, SATURDAY, FEBRUARY 22, 1862.   PRICE FOUR CENTS.

Confederate Army father breaks in on star-crossed lovers in a popular Boston Civil War-era weekly

During the Civil War, like many songs and stories of the time, some valentines reflected the poignancy and romance of lovers separated by the conflict. The tent valentine pictured here opens to reveal a Union officer at his camp desk writing with a quill pen to his sweetheart or wife. The verse reads:

TRUE JOY

My heart's not lightest
In hours of glee
My thoughts are brightest
When thinking of thee.

Yet this was also the mid-Victorian age, when English and American gentlemen handed women of the upper social classes onto pedestals and idolized them, when mothers and families were idealized (think of *Little Women*), when ironclad rules governed behavior, and when—next to honor—image and facade were all.

Civil War woodcut valentine shows
Yankee soldier and sweetheart

Sweet converse 'tis when lovers meet,
And all their vows renew,
And sweet the kiss with which they greet
Their fondness pure and true.

Hidden verse on this mid-Victorian embossed valentine, c. 1860s, reads: "Constant in hope / Constant in love / Constant to thee / All others above."

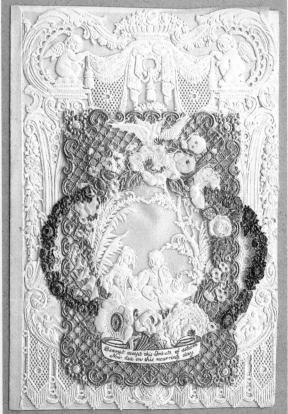

54

My dear little children,
How happy are they;
As fresh as Spring blossoms,
They gambol and play.
ST. VALENTINE'S morning
Shall bring to them joys;
There s always a blessing,
For good girls and boys.

The designers of mid- and late-Victorian valentines took their cue from the overheated, highly decorated parlors and drawing rooms of the day, heavy with velvet draperies, brocade upholstery, ornately carved furniture, glass-shaded lamps, urns full of ferns or peacock feathers, and fringe on everything. Besides the traditional lace, ribbons, and painted flowers, Victorian valentines dripped with seashells, feathers, silk or cambric flowers, satin leaves, moss wreaths, bits of seaweed, butterflies, and assorted trinkets. So heavily adorned were some cards that they required a box to hold them.

8-1/2 x 11" "boxed valentine," with layers so heavily adorned it required a box, has two layers of silver paper lace, pink satin ribbon, elaborate inside illustration, 1895-1900

Rare winter-scene valentine by Jotham Taft, 1880-85, includes Howland-style colored wafers and verse slip, a scroll that unwinds to read: "May happiness be always thine / No stormy days, but all sunshine."

New England designer Esther Howland added a touch of winter to 1882 card

LOVE
With His
Unerring Dart
HAS
PIERCED
my
True and Faithful

Victorian folding lace card by Kershaw & Sons, rice-paper center, cambric pansies, beads, pearls, ferns, gauze flower, gold leaf, 1870s

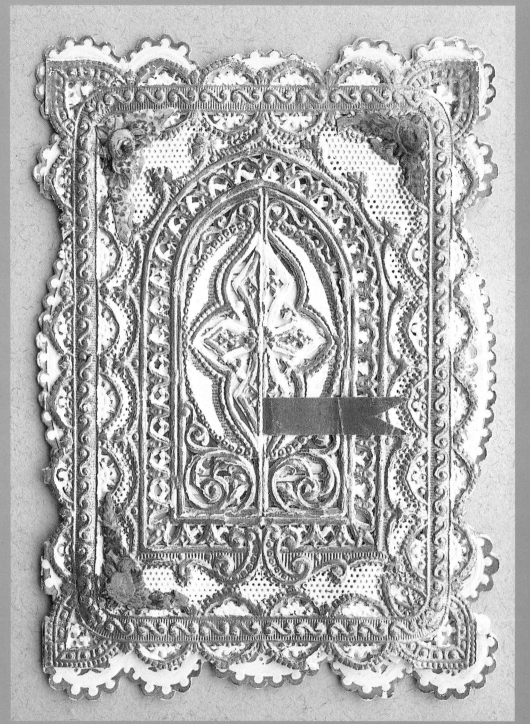

Verse behind church doors of Whitney valentine reads: "Words alone cannot unfold / The love I bear for thee / For thou art more precious far / Than costly gems to me"

Four-layered Whitney valentine, c. 1870

By the time Esther Howland sold her company in the early 1880s to George C. Whitney, another designer, it was bringing in a healthy hundred thousand a year, respectable for any business of the time and particularly remarkable for one owned by a woman. Whitney had been making valentines since the 1850s, and the Whitney name would appear on greeting cards for nearly a century, until World War II. His early designs, like Howland's, were lavish creations of lace, stick-ons, cupids, birds, flowers, and lovers. Whitney marked the 1870 example here, like all of his cards, with a red W and designed it especially for childhood sweethearts. Its verse reads:

> *In childhood*
> *when our hearts were young,*
> *A tender feeling 'tween us sprung,*
> *Which makes me send*
> *these lines to you*
> *To tell you I continue true.*

The gold foil and lace cards pictured are typical of Whitney's ornate Victorian designs around 1880.

For decades designers had offered a splendid variety of embellishments that buyers could glue on or send with their valentines to add a personal touch. These included die-cut pictures, or *scrap*, as well as stick-ons, called *swags*, and small personal greetings, often commemorative scenes like the portrait of President Grover Cleveland shown here. By the late nineteenth century, swags were often German imports and ranged from cupids and bouquets of paper flowers to colorful butterflies.

Swags, scrap, and personal greeting inserts, c. 1885-early 1900s—some of these swags retain paper tabs used to join them in sheets.

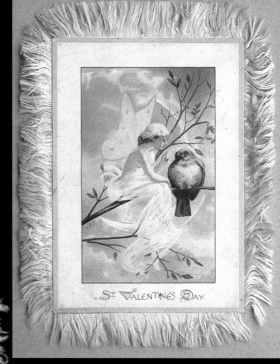

Prang silk-fringed card, 1883

MY LOVE
ACCEPT MY LOVE, TIS ALL

To the already lush Victorian valentines, London perfumer Eugene Rimmel added perfumed sachets. The flowery scents wafting from his manufactory drew passersby to his shop at 96 Strand, its windows bright with eye-pleasing displays of novelty cards and decorations. Rimmel tucked the cards with their pouchlike sachets, perfumed with lavender or violet absorbed into cotton wool, into lacy silver and gold envelopes so laden with embellishments no room remained for writing a name or address. Anyone sending one of these elaborate valentines had to deliver it by hand.

Other novelty valentines of the late nineteenth century included fan-shaped cards, cards with fringe or tassels, hold-to-the-light cards, and mock cablegrams. A German immigrant, Louis Prang, would become best known as a designer of Christmas cards but created quite elegant valentines as well.

Late 1800s card by Louis Prang

Perfumed sachet and satin-finish envelope with moveable maiden, feathers, satin leaves, by Rimmel, 1880s

P rang's countryman and contemporary Ernest Nister also produced novelty valentines in great demand in England and America, as did another German, Raphael Tuck.

Held to the light, patterns on folded Nister card merge to form image of a man and woman kissing, 1880s

THE SAILOR'S ADIEU.

"BIRDIE HAS COME."

1879

Tokens of Love

A single rose…chocolates…a heart-shaped trinket box…a lace handker-chief…all timeless tokens of love. Yet each era creates its own, and for Victorians, handcrafted gifts held special meaning. On long voyages, sailors carved stay busks, used as corset stiffeners, from wood or whalebone. And they made scrimshaw keepsakes, etching hearts and flowers, initials and sea scenes into bone. In the mid-nineteenth century, sailors to the British West Indies collected shells or bought them from native West Indians and, during idle hours on the voyage home, created delicate shell-mosaic valentines. Women often enclosed locks or small braids of hair in valentines and letters. Some designed elaborate picture frames, like the star frame shown here, which was created by winding darning thread around cardboard.

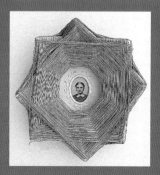

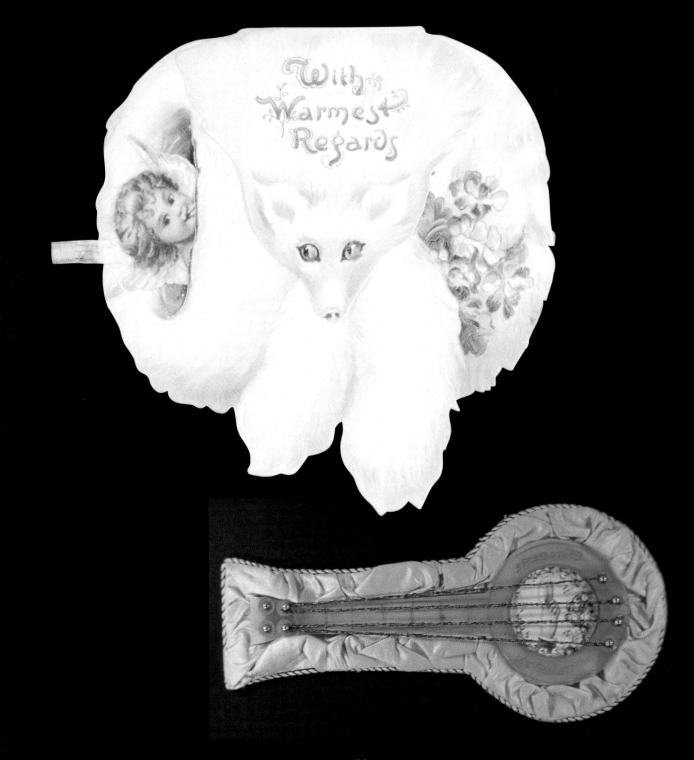

Nothing escaped the eye or pen of these novelty-card designers. They were equally inspired by satin banjos and fur muffs, and lent their talents to elaborate and loving varieties of certificates and awards.

Tuck & Sons fan with tasseled cord, c. 1880-90

Reward of merit from teacher to pupil, c. 1890

Five-layered rare heart-shaped card, 7-1/2 x 10", 1897

Victorian valentines layered with foil, flowers, children, cupids

Wilt thou be mine? dear love, reply,
Sweet consent, or else deny:
Whisper softly, none shall know,
Wilt thou be mine, love? ay or no?

By the gaslight era of the 1890s—the late Victorian period—the typical valentine consisted of a folded sheet overlain by an embossed lithograph, topped with fancy lace, often decorated with die-cut pictures. Paper springs made many cards three dimensional.

However colorful, life in the Gay Nineties was, for lovers, as fraught with doubt as any other decade. The verse inside the lacy scalloped peach-colored valentine here reads:

> *Ah! could I divine the secrets*
> *of your heart;*
> *In all its dreams of loving,*
> *could I know if I have part!*
> *Your words I hear,*
> *your smiles I see,*
> *Yet cannot read my destiny!*
>
> *The secret I do long to know;*
> *Beloved! pray thee tell,*
> *The secret, if you love me, who have*
> *loved you long and well.*
> *Beloved one, whisper unto me—*
> *Is joy or grief my destiny?*

Of Postcards and Prosperity

To my Sweet Valentine.

My hope, my heaven, my trust must be, My gentle guide, in following thee.

Greetings Sincere.

Will sing of your smile's bewitching power, Your every grace that warms and blesses, Will sing of your brow's luxuriant flower, The beaming glory of your tresses.
Moore

Gibson Girl card reads:
"Will sing of your smile's
bewitching power
Your every grace that warms
and blesses,
Will sing of your brow's
luxuriant flower,
The beaming glory of your tresses."

ibson Girls, croquet, and President William McKinley gave way with the turn of the century to Kewpie dolls, automobiles, and President Teddy Roosevelt. With the queen's death in 1903 the Victorian era officially ended, but for awhile valentines remained reassuringly bedecked with flowers, beautiful children, doves, and lace. Wall-hanging valentines, or "charm strings," became popular, with as many as seven pieces attached on one string.

Music-lover's wall-hanging card, 1910-15

Charm string over 18" long, hangs
by tassel, early 1900s

*Card's many elements are
all hand glued, possibly
from a kit, c. 1900*

To my
dear
Valentine
with
Love's
Greeting.

My Wish:
"Be True"
as I'm to you.

Valentine postcards,
1907-1910

To my
Valentine

A postcard craze struck the United States in the early 1900s. People scribbled "Wish you were here" on cards from the boardwalk in Atlantic City and the Eiffel Tower, from the Grand Canyon and the canals of Venice. On Valentine's Day and every other holiday they bombarded each other with postcard greetings. Everyone sent everyone else postcards, and everyone collected them, compared them, and pasted them in scrapbooks and postcard albums.

A valentine bookmark

Single-sheet lampoon, c.1910

On 1906 Valentine's Day dance program, partners could sign up for a waltz, schottische, two-step, quadrille, duchess, pan-American, gallop, or Portland fancy

Valentine postcards, 1907-1910

I WISH for you, a little man,
With manners always beautiful;
With clothing always spic and span,
His pleasure to be dutiful.
And if you're sharp, you will agree:
The portrait is describing me.
Your Valentine.

What means this shoe so very new?
Why, "23" skidoo, skidoo!

But if you'll be my Valentine,
This shoe, my love, will not fit you.

The Language of Gloves

For centuries, a gift of gloves from a man to a woman has tokened romance, perhaps because of the intimacy of glove to hand. London diarist Samuel Pepys recorded that Sir William Batten sent his wife "silk stockings, garters and a dozen pair of gloves" on February 14, 1661. As recently as the Victorian era, a woman might signal her acceptance of a man as her suitor by wearing to church the gloves he had sent her.

COURTESY OF THE MANCHESTER HISTORICAL SOCIETY, MANCHESTER-BY-THE-SEA, MASS.

Valentine postcards, 1907-1910

To my Valentine.
In these blue forget-me-nots,
In these fragrant roses too,
Read the message fond and true
From my faithful heart to you

At the other end of the scale from the simple valentine postcard were the German imports, popular from the 1890s until the mid-1930s. These magnificent stand-up cards composed of layer upon layer of chromolithographs were called "mechanical valentines" because of their moving parts. Depending on their construction, they were either "pull-downs" or "pull-outs."

*German pull-out valentine
more than a foot high, 1912*

To my Valentine

*German-engineered "mechanical"
pull-outs and pull-downs*

*Like American valentines,
German pull-down features
innocent youth*

In the years before World War I, valentines showed the effects of America's economic worries, with coarser lace, fewer layers, and little or no embossing.

Still, valentine writers held the romantic standard high, as in this typical verse from a 1912 card:

My peace with
wild emotion's torn,
From morn to eve,
from eve till morn.
And would you, fair one,
care to know
The reason why I languish?
Tis you who've cost me
all this woe,
This heart-ache and this anguish.
For dear, I love you deep and true,
And ne'er shall cease
to think of you.

These were hallmark years for American valentines, literally and figuratively. In 1906, a Polish immigrant, Jacob Sapirstein, founded American Greetings in Cleveland. The business that he started from postcards and a horse-drawn wagon is today one of the giants in the field, along with Hallmark, which opened its doors as Hall Brothers in 1910 in Kansas City, Missouri.

Stitching cupid, c.1920

Prewar economic measures included coarser lace of this early school-exchange valentine, 1912

World War I American soldier at French cafe pines for his sweetheart, blind to the charms of mademoiselle

During World War I, valentines reflected both the paper shortage and a yearning for more innocent times, at home and "over there." The cards often pictured servicemen as children, or at least as childlike, and the planes, ships, and army tents shown with them look more like toys than like the trappings of war.

Wartime souvenir, c.1916

When Cupid went to war, valentines got simpler, more innocent, c.1918

TO MY VALENTINE

choolmates and children began exchanging commercial valentines in the early 1900s. By the late thirties, as February 14 approached, in schoolrooms across the country a huge box appeared on the teacher's desk, decorated with red and white construction paper, crepe-paper ruffles, lace, and valentines, and with a slot in the top for children to drop cards in. On Valentine's Day, the teacher drew out the valentines one by one, read off the recipient's name, and handed the cards to runners to deliver to their schoolmates' desks. While the custom thrilled popular children, it caused many young hearts pain and anguish.

Soft-hearted woman lampooned in penny dreadful, 1920s

Many school-exchange
valentines had moving
parts—eyes, arms, mouths.

It is no "Puppy Love" I feel,
But something more divine.
So if you feel the self same way,
Then be my Valentine

Some school-exchange valentines came in pairs, to appeal to both boys and girls.

School-exchange valentines for the box on teacher's desk

Spooning

Spooning in June under the light of the moon—this term for kissing and amorous behavior in general may stem from an old Welsh custom in which an engaged man carved an ornate set of spoons for his fiancee. A thread run through a hole in the handle allowed her to wear them around her neck, and the couple would be known as "two spoons." The custom may have inspired Nister's chromolithograph of spoons in the 1880s, and surely the spirit of spooning animates this school exchange valentine from the 1930s-1940s.

Hall Brothers card with seven layers, ribbon applied by hand, c. 1936

The 1930s also brought cards made especially for wives, husbands, sweethearts, or parents, like the one pictured here decorated with silver foil and a pink satin bow. Its verse reads:

I used to think, "Boy, what a girl!"
whenever you were near,
I used to think there never was a
person quite so dear!
I used to like the things you said!
The way you said them too!
I used to think that you were swell!
And dearest, I still do!!

Fifteen-cent valentine by Rust Craft, now a subsidiary of American Greetings, c. 1937

During World War II, valentines again crisscrossed the Atlantic, and this time the Pacific as well, along with letters and postcards intended to raise spirits and comfort hearts at home and overseas.

MOTHER'S-HOME LIFE
and The HOUSEHOLD GUEST

FEBRUARY   1938

LITTLE THINGS LIKE VALENTINES
by HAZEL GOSSETT BASS

SUE wasn't sure when she had first become conscious of this utter lack of elation at her success, this feeling of futility and discontent, but she did know that the myriad displays of valentines had had a lot to do with the way she felt this morning. Foolish, gay, frivolous things—she had even dreamed about them last night.

Only, in her dreams, instead of the gorgeous paper lace creations, they had been heart shaped bits of pasteboard—gay, with smaller red hearts pierced with arrows, and pretty pictures with silly, treasured verses on them, "Roses are red, violets blue....," and "The world is wide and you can't step it....," and one was a beautiful beyond words lily with a baby in its heart, and hearts and cherubs around it, the one sister had made for her when she was nine, cutting the pictures from magazines; and they had been all tangled in her waking thoughts this morning. Oh! Not just the valentines, of course.

home. She had forgotten to remember that a mansion could not replace the home where their roots

NOMINATED THE CAMP'S MOST "POPULAR GUY"

CANDY

AC-13

To My Valentine

The captain on the battle ship,
Must watch the foe in rain or shine;
I too, must watch to get a glimpse
Of you, my Darling Valentine.

Women's Army Corps valentine
has moveable parts, 1940s

Lampoon valentine typical of 1949-50

Postwar prosperity and lightheartedness carried into the 1950s—women who had worked in plants and factories during the war went home to raise the kids, make apple pies, and decorate their ranchhouses in the new suburbs. But anyone, male or female, at home or not, was fair game for the so-called comic valentines of the day. One book of eleven cards that sold for ten cents lampooned gossipers, tightwads, card sharps, reckless drivers, housewives, baby-sitters, grasping Gerties, super salesmen, television hogs, sourpusses, and mambo dancers.

But whether fashioned from elaborate gold leaf and embossing or red construction paper and crayon, most valentines continue to echo the messages they have carried for hundreds of years: I love you. Do you love me? I'm yours. Be mine.

Gold Hallmark card, twenty-five cents in 1950s

Remembrance

I think of thee when soft and wide
The evening spreads her robes of light.
And like a young and timid bride
Sits blushing in the arms of night.
And when the moon's sweet crescent springs
Its light o'er heaven's deep waveless sea,
And stars are forth like blessed things,
I think of thee! I think of thee!

—From an 1890s valentine

References

I found the following books and sources invaluable: Edna Barth's *Hearts, Cupids, and Red Roses* (New York: Clarion); Cynthia Hart, John Freeman, and Tracy Gill's *Forget Me Nots* (New York: Workman); Frank Staff's *The Valentine and Its Origins* (New York: Praeger); and especially Ruth Webb Lee's *A History of Valentines* (Wellesley Hills, Mass.: Lee). I also found helpful information in the annual reports, publicity materials, and newsletters from American Greetings, Gibson Greetings, Inc., and Hallmark Cards, and from the International Collector's Society, Baltimore, Md.

PHOTOGRAPHIC CREDITS:

Len Wickens, pages 3, 8a, 10c, 11, 12, 14, 16, 17a, 20, 21b, 22, 23, 24b, 27, 28, 30a-b, 31, 32, 33a & c, 34b, 35-41, 44a, 45b, 46, 47a & c-d, 48, 49, 50b, 51, 52a, 54b, 55, 57a-b, 58-65, 67, 70b, 71, 73-75, 78a, 79, 80, 81b, 82-87, 89, 90b, 91-95, 97, 98, 99b, 101a, 103-106, 109, 110.

Paul Smith, pages 2, 8b, 10a-b, 13, 15, 17b, 18, 19, 21a, 24a, 25, 26, 29, 30c, 33b, 34a, 42, 43, 44b, 45a, 47b, 50a, 52b, 53, 54a, 56, 57c, 66, 68, 69, 70a, 72, 76, 77, 78b, 81a, 88, 90a, 96, 99a, 100, 101b, 102, 107, 108, 111.